To the World's Best
International Health Systems
Development Management Team.

A reminder to smell the roses
in the Kingdom.

Peter Colles
October 8, 1993

Jeddah
OLD AND NEW

Jeddah
OLD AND NEW

STACEY
INTERNATIONAL

The Publishers wish to acknowledge the invaluable
help of Robert Matthew, Johnson-Marshall & Partners,
the practice of architects, city planners and engineers
who are advisers to the Municipality on the preservation
of historic Jeddah.

Jeddah Old and New
First published in 1980
Reprinted 1981
Revised edition 1991
Stacey International
128 Kensington Church Street,
London w8 4BH
Telex 298768 STACEY G

ISBN 0 905743 64 4

Textual preparation
James Buchan

Editorial research & direction
Engineer Zaki Farsi
George Duncan
Amr Darwish
Dr John Russell
Hassan Dajani
Dr Abbas Yehia

Picture research
Anna Dowson
Charlotte Breese

Design
Anthony Nelthorpe MSIAD
Keith Savage

Special drawings
W. Spencer Tart

Cartography:
Peter Cannings

Set in Ehrhardt by SX Composing Limited,
Rayleigh, Essex, England
Colour origination, printing and binding by
Dai Nippon Printing Company, Tokyo, Japan

All photographs of "Historic Jeddah" were taken by
John French, and all photographs of "Jeddah Today
and Tomorrow" were taken by **Khalid Khidr**, except
those listed below. Page numbers and quantity of
photographs, if more than one, follow the photographer's
name. Asterisks denote line drawings.
Aga Khan Award for Architecture, 94–95;
Carl Byoir and Associates Inc., 142; Kit Constable-
Maxwell, 2–3, 79, 81, 90–91, 91(2), 92, 93, 94–95, 100,
100–101, 101(2), 102–103, 106(2), 108, 111, 112,
113(2), 116, 118–119, 126–127, 129; Alistair Duncan,
Middle East Photographic Archive (MEPhA), 123;
George Duncan, 106–107, 107(2), 113(2); Mel Evans,
79, 80, 82(2), 84(2), 86(2), 87, 88(2), 92(2), 104–105,
105(3), 106, 107, 109, 111, 115(3), 119, 120(3), 121, 122,
123, 128, 133; Gunter Fischer, 84, 84–85(2); IAP, 6–7;
Sert Jackson, 26–27, 36–37, 41, 48, 49, 52, 53–54, 53, 54,
55, 58(2), 58–59, 59(2), 72, 74–75; IAP/Kevin Haupt &
Steve Tom, 96–97(4), 142–3(3); Jeddah Municipality,
12; Shirley Kay, John Topham Picture Library, 122;
Robert Matthew, Johnson-Marshall and Partners, 21(2),
22(2), 22–23, 115(2), 116, 118(2), 119, 121; T. Mostyn,
Middle East Photographic Archive (MEPhA), 115;
News Afro-Asian Service (NAAS), 98(2), 98–99;
Anthony Nelthorpe, 66, 82–83; Owens/Corning
Fiberglas Corporation, 79, 144; Popperfoto, 97; P.
Ryan, Middle East Photographic Archive (MEPhA),
80(2); Samarec, 120; Saudia, 143; Spencer Tart, 10*(2), 14*,
15*, 17, 78, 80, 85, 111, 115, 136*(2), 137*(2), 138*(2), 139*,
140–141*; Umdasch, 112; Visnews, 98.

Contents

Foreword

My responsibility and my concern are twofold – for the dynamic growth of a flourishing modern city, and for the preservation of the religious, social and environmental attributes of our ancient, Islamic, Arab Jeddah, "Bride of the Red Sea".

It is not enough to plan, organise and monitor the development of a major city. The quality of life and of the place itself are central to the scheme of things. I am reminded of Ibn Khaldun, six centuries ago: "The purpose of cities is to provide a place to build and to give shelter. One must keep out what is harmful and bring in what is useful. . . . The craft of architecture is the first and oldest craft of sedentary civilisation."

For me it is a ceaseless challenge – too great for a single man. My

This foreword to the first edition of *Jeddah Old and New* was written in 1980.

gratitude goes out to H.M. King Khalid bin Abdul Aziz and H.R.H. the Crown Prince Fahd bin Abdul Aziz for their wise counsel and constant encouragement, as also to H.R.H. Prince Majid bin Abdul Aziz, former Minister for Municipal and Rural Affairs and now the Emir of the Mecca Region.

Special thanks are also due to our Municipality staff for their loyalty and dedication.

By the grace of God, their efforts have combined to cope with the tremendous pressures of rapid growth, and the improvement, beautification and renewal of the city.

It gives me great pleasure to introduce this portrait of the city of Jeddah – Jeddah old, and Jeddah new.

Eng. Mohamed Said Farsi
MAYOR OF JEDDAH 1973–1986

Jeddah
OLD AND NEW

JEDDAH is a city-port of great age: the gateway to Holy Makkah and western Arabia, "Bride of the Red Sea". Confined for several centuries by its desert hinterland and an uncertain water supply within massive walls of bleached coral, Jeddah's population has grown some sixtyfold in the two generations to the present day.

In the 1940s the walls were torn down. With them went Jeddah's old identity, as the town began to advance across sand, saltmarsh and coral reef into a sprawling modern city. It is still growing as Saudi Arabians move in from the hinterland to settle in modern homes, and as foreigners take up temporary residence to play their part in the country's vigorous growth.

Jeddah today is thus a city of striking variety: seascape and cityscape, the ancient amid the modern, the elegant amid the garish; a city of alleys and boulevards, of an aspect sometimes utilitarian and sometimes aesthetic. Despite the contrasts, Jeddah has held to a distinctive Arab character—and in faithfulness to this Arab essence, displays a living green against the parched dun of the surrounding landscape.

To manage Jeddah is an awesome, costly task.

The city is situated about half way along the Red Sea's eastern coast. Jeddah owes its existence to the presence of a gap in the triple line of coral reefs fringing the Red Sea shore and to another gap in the Great Arabian Massif barrier which allowed communications – via the Wadi Fatima – inland to Makkah.
Arab geographers report legends that Eve began her search for Adam at Jeddah (or, according to some, returned to the town from Paradise), and that she is buried there.

The nucleus of the city began to form at the north end of a bay so encumbered with banks of reefs that it seems strange that such an inhospitable anchorage on the coast of Arabia should have become a busy seaport. To be sure, a small settlement existed from the very earliest times, but it was when the cities of the Mediterranean gained a taste for incense from South Arabia and ship-borne spices and luxuries from the East that the town started to grow. The ancient town's Persian masters were obliged to dig three hundred or more wells and cisterns in the sixth century C.E.* With the coming of Islam at the beginning of the seventh century, the port's significance was assured for all time.

Yet even as the principal port for pilgrims to Makkah – a mere forty-seven miles inland in a bowl of barren hills – Jeddah does not appear

*Christian Era, *i.e.* A.D.

to have been first choice. The landing for Makkah was at Shuaiba, at the south of the bay, until the Caliph Uthman was called in to find a harbour safer from pirates in the twenty-sixth year of the Islamic era (646–647). Qutb Al-Din tells that the Caliph bathed in the sea at Jeddah and liked it. Nowadays, well over one million pilgrims arrive through Jeddah's airport and harbour every year, from every corner of the Islamic world.

At first, Jeddah found itself the main port

In this engraving of Jeddah (c. 1854) some have identified the minaret on the right as that of Masjid Hanefi, surviving today.

for the expanding Arab empire. With the transfer of the Caliphate northwards—to Baghdad and Damascus—Jeddah retained a hold on the profitable Red Sea spice trade. The Persian poet, Naser Khusrow, visited the town in 1050 and left the first written account. He describes a thriving place:

"Jeddah is a great city surrounded by a strong wall, with a population of some five thousand males. The bazaars are fine. There are no trees or any vegetation at all, but all that is necessary for life is brought in from surrounding villages."

The mounting sea power of Europe threatened this prosperity. The circumnavigation of Africa by Vasco da Gama in the later fifteenth century turned Portuguese eyes to the rich opportunities of the eastern trade. A former dependant of the Mamluk Sultan of Egypt, Hussein Al-Kurdi, styled himself governor of Jeddah and rebuilt the walls of the town. They withstood a Portuguese attack and blockade. But in 1517, the town fell under the power of the Ottoman Turks, as part of

the domain of the Sharif of Mecca.

As the Portuguese, Dutch and English began to monopolize trade, Jeddah ceased to be a commercial *entrepôt* of importance and subsided into its traditional role as a pilgrim port. It continued to act as a transit point for commerce between Egypt and India, but it was in a dilapidated state when visited by the Danish expedition under Carsten Niebuhr in 1761:

"The walls are still standing but are now so ruinous that a person may, in many places, enter over them on horseback. In the city, however, there are several fine buildings of coral stone. The city is entirely destitute of water. The inhabitants have none to drink but what is collected by Arabs in reservoirs among the hills and brought thence on camels."

In the early nineteenth century, Turkish rule was interrupted, first by the Saudis of Central Arabia and then by the Egyptians, but the Turks were back in partnership with the Sharif by 1840. As the India trade expanded, the European powers established consulates in a special quarter just inside the northern gates. Jacob Burckhardt, the Swiss traveller, describes the arrival of the India fleet on the May monsoon as a time of intense excitement. The Jeddah merchants "having collected as many dollars and sequins as their circumstances

admit, effect bargains at wholesale at the first arrival of the ships". With all liquidity soaked up, the town came to a standstill until the departure of the fleet in July, "when it commonly occurs that, on the very day the last ships sail, ten per cent profit may be obtained on the first price". During the fleet's idleness, lascars engaged in fashioning the intricate doors and screens that are the loveliest features of old Jeddah houses today.

Resentment in the Muslim world at the growing European control, which flared up in the Indian Mutiny in 1858, did not completely bypass Jeddah; a group of consuls and traders strolling by the Manqabah Lagoon just north of the town were set upon and the English, unsatisfied with the Pasha's investigation, sent the British naval ship *Cyclops* to bombard the town. A shell landing on the sea-front caused the minaret of the Al-Basha Mosque to lean like

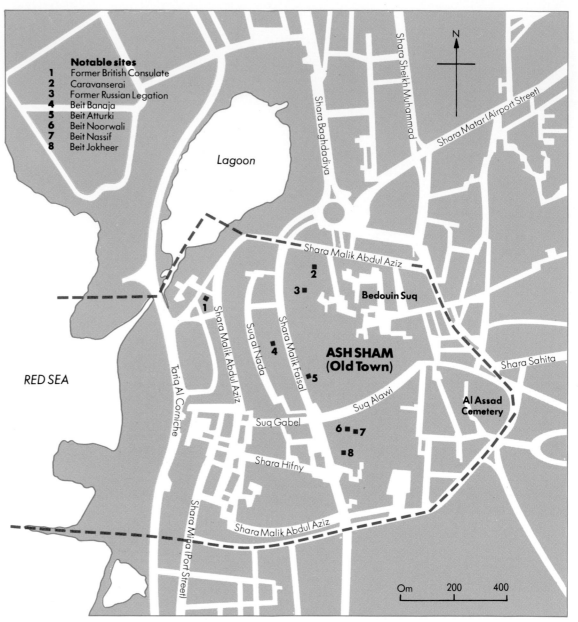

Al-Basha Mosque, with its once famous tilted minaret.

the Tower of Pisa, providing Jeddah with one of its most celebrated landmarks until its demolition in 1979.

The opening of the Suez Canal in 1869 proved a boon for Jeddah and, by the turn of the century, its merchants of Hadhrami, Javanese or Indian origin were handling a regular volume of commerce with other Arabian ports, India, Egypt, and Africa and even Liverpool and Marseilles.

From this period date the many fine merchant family houses that survive in the old city. The most celebrated of such houses— and justly so, for its fine appearance and state of preservation—is Beit Nassif (Nassif House), on Al Alawi Street, home of the Nassif family for over a century, until the house was passed to the care of the Government in the mid 1970s. Designed by a Jeddah master-builder of the day, it is built of coral limestone tied by teak beams, and contains fifty high-ceilinged rooms. The coral blocks are bound by a mortar whose base is date pulp. It was here

Notable sites
1 Former British Consulate
2 Caravanserai
3 Former Russian Legation
4 Beit Banaja
5 Beit Atturki
6 Beit Noorwali
7 Beit Nassif
8 Beit Jokheer

Above The dotted line encloses the area designated for conservation and restoration.

The original Bab Makkah, the Makkah gate – drawn from a photograph of the 1920s.

that King Abdul Aziz bin Abdul Rahman al Sa'ud ("Ibn Saud") stayed during his early visits to the city.

Another such house, Beit Banaja, is entered by way of the Suq Al Nada, just to the east of King Abdul Aziz Street. Its finely carved pair of wooden doors open behind two market stalls. Parts of this great house pre-date the nineteenth century. The thick stone walls and louvred shutters keep the house relatively cool without air-conditioning. From such a many-chambered edifice the whole extensive and well-ordered family would carry on its varied business during the nineteenth century—and indeed, up to the middle of the present century.

In 1910, the port of Jeddah's export trade was only worth £65,000, mostly in the hides and skins that are still Saudi Arabia's second largest export. But imports, partly financed by the spending of pilgrims, were as high as £1,750,000. A portion of this was for transit, but the largest items were grain and rice to feed the pilgrims and to meet the growing demand of the interior.

In *Seven Pillars of Wisdom*, T. E. Lawrence describes a walk from the Customs' Quay to the British Legation in the north in 1916:

"It was indeed a remarkable town. The streets were alleys, wood roofed in the main bazaar, but elsewhere open to the sky in the little gap between the tops of the lofty white-walled houses. These were built four or five storeys high, the coral rag tied with square beams and decorated by wide bow-windows running from ground to roof in grey wooden panels. There was no glass in Jeddah but a profusion of good lattices and some very delicate shallow chiselling on the panels of window casings. The doors were heavy two-leaved slabs of teak-wood, deeply carved, often with wickets in them; and they had rich hinges and riggknockers of hammered iron.

"There was much moulded or cut plastering and on the older houses fine stone heads and jambs to the windows looking on the inner courts. . . . . . housefronts were fretted, pierced and pargetted till they looked as though cut out of cardboard for a romantic stage setting. Every storey jutted, every window leaned one way or another; often

In a unique photograph, life in the commercial heart of old Jeddah is recaptured in the 1920s.

the very walls sloped.

"It was like a dead city, so clean underfoot and so quiet . . . . The atmosphere was oppressive, deadly. One would say that for years, Jeddah had not been swept by a firm breeze."

There was little outside the walls. Apart from the Turkish barracks, known as the Qishla and still standing to the east of the lagoon, the fishing village of Ruwais beyond the coral quarries to its west, and the little desert settlement of Bani Malik, the only settlement of any size was the sprawling mud village of Nakatu to the south, home of poor West African pilgrims.

That year—1916—Sharif Hussein of Makkah, encouraged by almost eleven million pounds in English gold, revolted against the Turks. But the Sharifian regime was short-lived; in central Arabia, a new generation of Saudis, moved by a powerful sense of religious destiny and the ability of Abdul Aziz "Ibn Saud", were now an

Shortly before Jeddah lost its city wall from 1947, the photograph below was taken from a northwesterly angle. The Bab Medina is seen at 1, and close to it Beit Bajnaid 2 and the caravanserai 3. Nearer to the sea stood the former British embassy 4, and on the sea itself was the site of the famous kindasah (water distilling machine) 5. Readers who know today's Jeddah will locate the Gabil Suq at 6.

Right *From the south west, Jeddah's wall is clearly visible in this earliest aerial photograph ever taken, with lagoon beyond.*

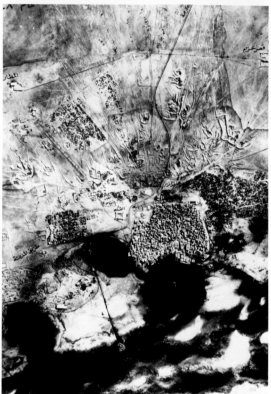

Above *As seen from the east in 1948, Jeddah Old Town, one and a half square kilometres, is seen spilling out southeast and, across the lagoon, northwards. The Makkah road stretches east.*

irresistible force. Hussein's son Ali attempted resistance. It was a makeshift military endeavour:

"Some abandoned American army lorries which a Syrian had picked up were fitted with thin metal sheeting and sold to the Hejaz Government for £2,300 apiece. One was driven out of the barbed-wire defences by a Russian refugee and shot through and through by the Saudis. The driver obtained £50 in compensation beside a post-dated cheque for another £50. He went to Egypt, gave a party for his Russian refugee friends and returned to Jeddah penniless."

The Saudis had control of the farms and wells of Wadi Fatima and the whole of the hinterland was behind them. After a siege in which old men in Jeddah today remember the poor begging for water, the town surrendered on December 23rd, 1925. The modern history of Jeddah begins from that day.

Curiously, for all Jeddah's varied history, the character of the town changed little between Naser Khusrow and the arrival of the Saudis.

The pilgrims came and, if they could afford it, went; ships still edged through the dangerous gateways between the three coral reefs; sweet water remained the perennial problem although by now a sea water distillation device, or condenser (Arabized as *kindasah*) north of the Customs Quay provided a few gallons of drinkable water every day.

Within Hussein Al-Kurdi's walls, the town grew upwards. The climate of Jeddah, its humidity, would hardly be tolerable but for the breeze that blows down from the north-west most days of the year. The coral houses reared upwards to catch the breeze while tight agglomerations of buildings created draughts. In the absence of any stone for paving, the streets and little squares were floored with fine sand.

At the centre of the town's life was the Customs Quay, where lighters and *sambuks* offloaded goods from the freighters in the bay. Just inland was the main street of the town and behind it a maze of alleys that formed the *suq*, protected from the sun by palm leaves and canvas and ringed on the south by Shara Sabil. It was as compact as a hive.

Visitors and pilgrims were housed in the caravanserais—rambling hostelries—clustered around the town's five main gates: Bab Mecca, Bab Medina, Bab El-Bunt at the quay, Bab Sharif and Bab Al-Maghribah. The growing diplomatic community took over the old *bilad Al-Kanasil* (the consul's quarter) inside Bab Medina, where the breeze was best.

With the Great Depression of the 1930s, the pilgrimage began to falter and the finances of Jeddah, and the state, were sorely strained. In May 1933, Abdul Aziz' finance minister, Al Sulaiman, signed an oil concession in Jeddah with the Standard Oil Company of California. Thirty-five thousand pounds in gold sovereigns were counted across a table in Jeddah. Five years later, oil began to flow in the Eastern Province and Jeddah's days as a walled city were numbered.

Immediately after the Second World War, the effects began to be felt. The walls were demolished, but at least the water problem receded with the piping of three million gallons a day from wells fifty miles to the south in Wadi Fatima ("Save us from the clamour of *kindasah*", the poet Mohammed Said Otaibi

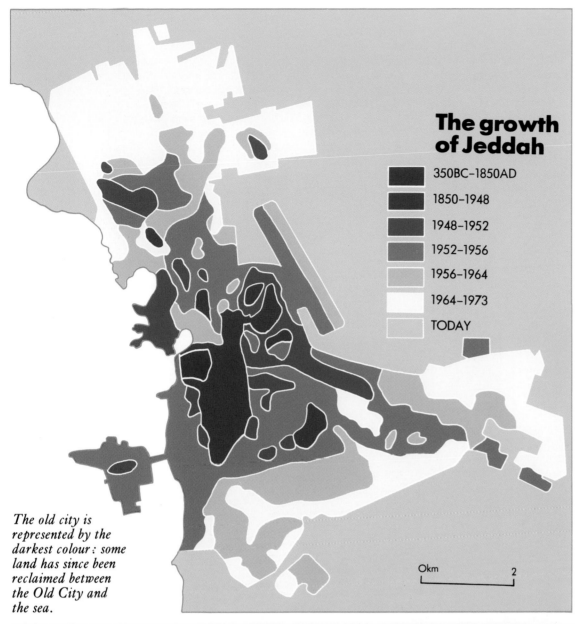

The growth of Jeddah

- 350BC–1850AD
- 1850–1948
- 1948–1952
- 1952–1956
- 1956–1964
- 1964–1973
- TODAY

The old city is represented by the darkest colour: some land has since been reclaimed between the Old City and the sea.

0km   2

recited at the dedication ceremony). A harbour with a broad channel was created to supplant the Customs Quay.

Confined to the east by the hills and wadis of the Hejaz range, and to the south by salt-marshes ablaze with flamingoes, the city broke out northwards in a rash of haphazard building along the Medina Road. Some order was restored with the growing experience of the Municipality in the 1960s, but the early pattern was repeated in aggravated form with the quadrupling of oil prices in 1973–1974. A master plan in 1973, which predicted a population of 1.6 million in 1990, was over-taken by the sheer numbers flooding into the town, and the inrush of new wealth.

The Pilgrimage and sea-borne trade have meant that Jeddah was always a cosmopolitan city, but for a hundred years up to 1945 the population had been stable at about twenty to thirty thousand; by 1971, the numbers had increased gradually to three hundred and fifty thousand; by 1980 they had leapt to nearly one million.

The Jeddah harbour, obliged to meet a demand for building materials and consumer goods from the whole country, was forced into superhuman effort. Whereas cargo offloaded in 1946 was a mere 150,000 tons, and in 1966 only just over one million tons, by 1977 ships were discharging over eight million tons a year. On some days a pall of cement dust hung over the town by day, while by night ships waiting to discharge were strung out like fairy lights twenty miles into the roads. Yet in that single year, with the volume of cargo constantly increasing, waiting was eliminated. Ships were arriving and tying up, and their cargo rolling off and cleared through the port, all in a matter of three days.

In the nine years following 1971, the number of cars in the city multiplied about twenty times, and with them the parking problems and traffic congestion where the radial streets of the old town met the grid pattern of the north. It was a challenge confronted by the radical introduction of single direction traffic, the building of major peripheral arteries—including between the city and the sea—the provision of extensive parking areas, and the vigorous activity of traffic police.

Far more serious, in the eyes of the Munici-pality, was the haphazard growth to the north and along the Makkah road as prices of land and property spiralled out of control. Every Jeddah family was tempted to see itself as a property developer. With ninety per cent of Jeddah land in private hands, the power of the city was limited. Acceptable land use practices became almost impossible to enforce, while construction was often of poor quality. Some of the finest old buildings in Jeddah disap-peared as the old town nearest the sea was redeveloped.

The caravanserai (khans) were havens of rest and security to traders and travellers after the hazards of sea and desert travel.

In these conditions, much of the energy of the then mayor, Mohamed Said Farsi, and of most other sectors of Government were consumed simply in providing services to keep pace with the boom.

Yet the Pilgrimage remained a priority and has been managed with increasing skill. In the past, Jeddah paid dearly for the privilege. There had been outbreaks of cholera (known piously as "the great mercy") or disasters like the fire that destroyed the *s.s. Asia* and all its pilgrims in 1929. Poor Hajjis who could not afford their lighterage to the Customs Quay, let alone the journey home, swelled the city's beggar community. These are all memories. Today's King Abdul Aziz Airport handles an aircraft every half a minute during the pilgrimage. At this immense new airport fifteen miles to the north, provision has been made for a million and a half pilgrims (as well as six million other passengers) each year.

The series of ring roads was planned to keep traffic flowing between jobs in the old town and new housing in the north. Simultaneously, a storm water channel was constructed to protect the town from the violent floods that once or twice a decade pour down the wadis from the basalt hills of the Hejaz. The problem of water supply was settled once and for all—one hopes—by the installation of four mighty desalination plants on a lagoon to the north, capable of providing eighty million gallons every day. The shards of the old *kindasah* have been erected as monuments along the road, to remind the future that it was not ever as easy.

For although social life, as reflected in the persistent division of guest and family space in new houses or in the demure picnicking along the Corniche, remained remarkably stable during the boom, the feel of the town changed. Many sensed that the glittering shops and apartment blocks had lost their sense of

Beit Bajnaid (photographed on pages 70 and 71), designated as one of the 550 buildings for rehabilitation, is seen below as it is today, with all its accretions, and opposite after proposed restoration to its original fine lines.

direction, petering out in dusty, vacant spaces and that the new town lacked solidity and permanence; beneath the cool flags of Jeddah's grand hotels, the desert sighed. It was inevitable, of course. Cities *need* time.

The Mayor, in particular, was concerned that the town's appearance did not sufficiently reflect Jeddah's place in Islam or history. It was turning its back on the sea, the source of all its prosperity. Above all, the human scale of small streets and minarets, and the familiar human textures of wood and paint, were vanishing fast amid the mass of glass and steel.

With the fierce development of recent years beginning to abate by the late 1970s, the Municipality was in a position to require certain standards from the people of Jeddah. It insisted that new building belonged recognizably to an Islamic tradition and it asked that materials other than the ubiquitous reinforced concrete of the early and mid 1970s be used. The results so far, particularly in the sought-after district of Hamra, have been decidedly promising.

At the heart of Jeddah, and of Jeddah's idea of itself, are the old houses of the walled town. The city has identified some one thousand traditional buildings of which five hundred and thirty-seven have been "listed" as of architectural and historical importance—grand merchants' palaces or clusters of smaller workers' houses, or buildings with unique or characteristic features in their doorways or windows or roof crenellations and so on—that

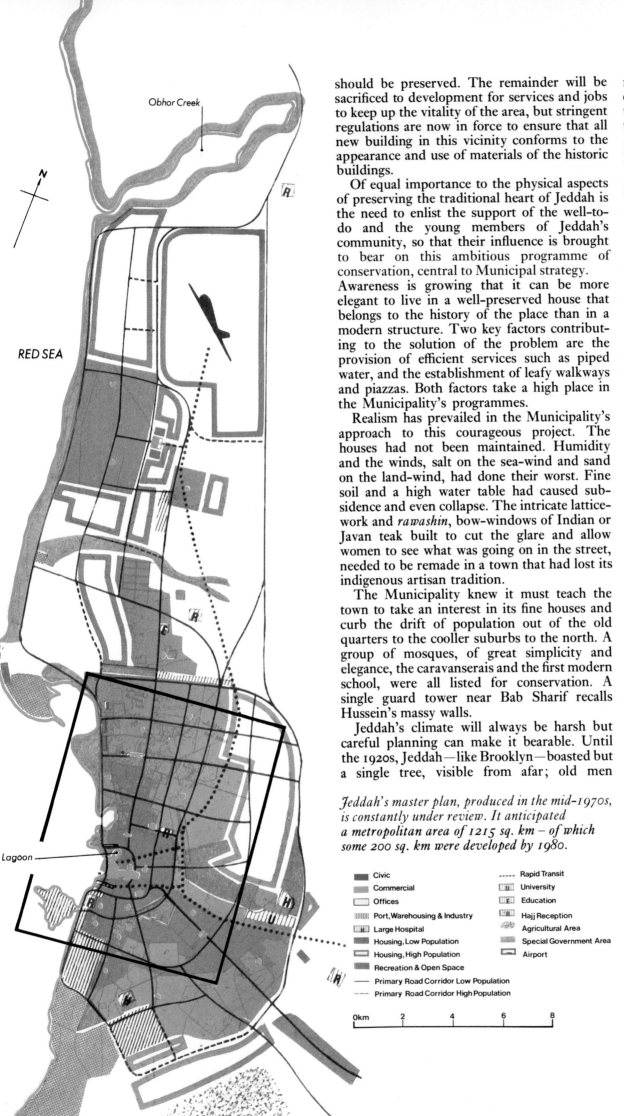

Obhor Creek

N

RED SEA

Lagoon

should be preserved. The remainder will be sacrificed to development for services and jobs to keep up the vitality of the area, but stringent regulations are now in force to ensure that all new building in this vicinity conforms to the appearance and use of materials of the historic buildings.

Of equal importance to the physical aspects of preserving the traditional heart of Jeddah is the need to enlist the support of the well-to-do and the young members of Jeddah's community, so that their influence is brought to bear on this ambitious programme of conservation, central to Municipal strategy. Awareness is growing that it can be more elegant to live in a well-preserved house that belongs to the history of the place than in a modern structure. Two key factors contributing to the solution of the problem are the provision of efficient services such as piped water, and the establishment of leafy walkways and piazzas. Both factors take a high place in the Municipality's programmes.

Realism has prevailed in the Municipality's approach to this courageous project. The houses had not been maintained. Humidity and the winds, salt on the sea-wind and sand on the land-wind, had done their worst. Fine soil and a high water table had caused subsidence and even collapse. The intricate lattice-work and *rawashin*, bow-windows of Indian or Javan teak built to cut the glare and allow women to see what was going on in the street, needed to be remade in a town that had lost its indigenous artisan tradition.

The Municipality knew it must teach the town to take an interest in its fine houses and curb the drift of population out of the old quarters to the cooler suburbs to the north. A group of mosques, of great simplicity and elegance, the caravanserais and the first modern school, were all listed for conservation. A single guard tower near Bab Sharif recalls Hussein's massy walls.

Jeddah's climate will always be harsh but careful planning can make it bearable. Until the 1920s, Jeddah—like Brooklyn—boasted but a single tree, visible from afar; old men

Jeddah's master plan, produced in the mid-1970s, is constantly under review. It anticipated a metropolitan area of 1215 sq. km – of which some 200 sq. km were developed by 1980.

■ Civic	----- Rapid Transit
■ Commercial	▦ University
□ Offices	▦ Education
▥ Port, Warehousing & Industry	▦ Hajj Reception
▦ Large Hospital	▨ Agricultural Area
□ Housing, Low Population	▨ Special Government Area
□ Housing, High Population	▭ Airport
■ Recreation & Open Space	
— Primary Road Corridor Low Population	
--- Primary Road Corridor High Population	

0km   2   4   6   8

remember it black with exhausted songbirds on their migration south. It still stands outside the great Nassif House in Shara Al Alawi, but the town today has grown green around it. *Neem* trees, gold *mohur*, and jacarandas provide shade and the pavements are planted with oleanders and *doum* palms; bougainvillaea, jasmine and hibiscus sprout over villa walls. The whole of Jeddah has grown green with some eight million trees.

The city has taken over thirty areas of former waste-ground for parks. After mixed results with grass and shrubs that strained resources in maintenance, the Municipality succeeded with a mixture of cacti, succulents and desert bushes that can tolerate a saline soil and little water. The emphasis is on shade.

None of the parks, or even the wholesale re-siting of industry downwind of the town, will do as much for the city in terms of fresh air as the Corniche project. Aware that, at least until the 1990s, nearly half of the population will be children, the city has taken over twenty miles of coastline solely for the purposes of providing recreation. From the Obhor Creek some fifteen miles to the north to as far south as Ras Al-Aswad, twenty miles beyond the city, all but those areas occupied by the port, the refinery or other installations are given over to recreation either organized into watersports at the northern lagoon or simply for picnicking. The first part of the northern section was complete by 1980, and, on holidays, the promenades are full of families and children. It is this grand imaginative gesture of road, promenade, parking area, trees and monuments that has brought back the sea decisively into the heart of the city.

Mayor Mohamed Said Farsi encouraged private businessmen to donate sculptures and monuments and fountains to the town and the corniche. They offer arresting and intriguing points of focus and the same imaginative touch that marks the best of the *rawashin*.

Jeddah has begun to capitalise on the flair displayed in its city beautification programme by embarking on an ambitious scheme to increase its appeal as a city of tourism, leisure and recreation.

The Abdul Raouf Hasan Khalif Museum provides a spectacular setting for the display of Jeddah's traditional past. Among projects in preparation are a zoo, an aquarium and marine life sanctuary, a central park with an artificial lake, restoration of the remaining parts of the old city, a motor racing track, restaurants and art galleries. Recreation projects are also planned for the mountains in the hinterland.

The grand and subtle intention of those controlling the city's destiny is that the peculiar qualities of Jeddah, its commerce and its sense of its own part in Islam will persist and that if Naser Khusrow returned he would recognize his great town and fine bazaars, only they will be larger, greener and better provided with water.

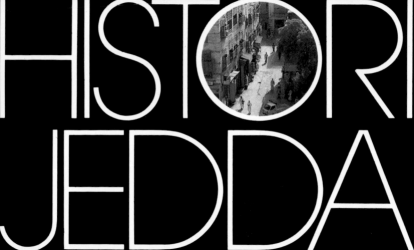

The year 1979 – when these pictures were taken – is already history for Jeddah. But they demonstrate the speed and method with which the city's ideas have been worked out. The reclaimed foreshore (far left) was, by 1980, a well-ordered parking area – for a city expected to contain 250 cars for every 1,000 of its 1.6 million inhabitants by 1990. Behind the modern facade (above) lies – unexpectedly – the old city, partly seen, containing the characteristically fine merchant's house, Beit Nassif (left).

One of the finest examples of architecture in
"Old" Jeddah, Nassif House, is a large
merchant's residence in the Alawi Suq. The
exquisite craftsmanship displayed in the carving,
fretwork, mouldings, mushrabiyah and fanlights
has been preserved and restored to its original
state. Mohammad Nassif, born in 1884 in
Jeddah, made a memorable collection of old
manuscripts and books and the building is now
in the public domain. Overleaf: Details of Beit
Nassif.

The originality of Beit Noorwali reaches to the very roof – in its confusion of levels, its toothed crenellations, and the pointed dome of its top-floor bathroom.

Until recently some merchants' fine houses, such as the example left, were in diplomatic use as legations and chancelleries. Known locally as khans, Jeddah's caravanserais (bottom far left and centre) where visitors sheltered, were celebrated among travellers as "sanctuaries and sacred places free from insults and robberies".

This small caravanserai (above) is now used as a home for elderly ladies. Its rare exterior illustrates arabesque design detailed directly on the plasterwork, unlike all other caravanserai in the city which are without ornamentation.

*Small traditional houses of two, three and four
storeys, built of coral limestone faced with lime
stucco and either white-washed or colour-
washed pastel shades, constitute the major part
of Jeddah's unique heritage of buildings of
architectural and historical significance.*

Small balconies with lattice screens (shish) and simple casements (mushrabiyah) are typical examples of the older surviving examples of traditional houses. The lack of simple routine maintenance is the largest single factor which contributed to the deterioration of Jeddah's heritage.

Galleries, balconies and bay windows (rawashin) *ornament another large merchant's house.*

The entrance door (left) and its arches demand some restoration, but still display original craftmanship.

Above *There are panel windows and an ornate fanlight in this smaller house which is in good condition.*

33

The detail (top) of carved wood panels on the east wall of a large merchant's house is typical of the care lavished by craftsmen on these buildings. Constructed of teak or similar hardwoods resistant to insect attack and high levels of relative humidity, rawashin *or bay windows (above and right) are striking features.*

The very tall houses catch the regular sea breezes and create upward draughts with their temperature differentials. The overhanging open-louvred windows filter the glare, but allow air to circulate freely in the rooms. The streets are purposely as narrow as possible to create the maximum shade.

This medium-sized merchant's house demonstrates fine carving, fretwork and latticework with skilfully cantilevered balconies. It also features ornately carved plasterwork on the lower storeys. The house still has its original carved door, beneath semi-circular, horseshoe and shallow arch headings and an unusual fanlight.

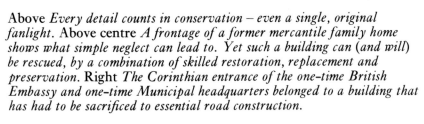

Above *Every detail counts in conservation – even a single, original fanlight.* **Above centre** *A frontage of a former mercantile family home shows what simple neglect can lead to. Yet such a building can (and will) be rescued, by a combination of skilled restoration, replacement and preservation.* **Right** *The Corinthian entrance of the one-time British Embassy and one-time Municipal headquarters belonged to a building that has had to be sacrificed to essential road construction.*

Bottom centre *a small traditional town house's doorway is a candidate for restoration.*

Bottom right *a window of the former Municipality headquarters.*

43

This charming courtyard containing several characteristic features in its windows (rawashin), fanlight, mouldings and ironwork, is customarily used for prayer.

For elegant bathing in historic Jeddah, no house could compete with Beit Noorwali (above), whose owners have carefully preserved the interiors from deterioration – as, for example, the majlis (top opposite). Right: the well of the house and right, opposite: the stairway.

Several traditional houses still overlook Baiya Square at the head of the lagoon – as, for example, that (left) facing the Jeddah Palace Hotel, once the French Embassy. Its loggias and balconies, casements and bay windows have been well preserved.

The small town house (bottom left) *retains several characteristics of old Jeddah in its* mushrabiyah *and* rawashin. *Bottom centre:* former Russian Legation. Right *This medium-sized town house, with much surviving woodwork, has five storeys.*

This merchant's house (left) is in unusually fine condition: the five-storeyed house (lower left) presents an impressive frontage of latticework and balconies and shallow arched headings. Lower right The six-storeyed large merchant's house has crenellated parapets and elegant casements. Above The coral blocks, which comprise the main material of Jeddah's traditional houses, are clearly visible.

The projecting timber windows served for observation, unseen, of the comings and goings below.

"Greetings Oh you seated in the latticed balcony
And exalted high above all the people." (*Popular couplet*).

The projecting loggia of the large merchant's house – Beit Al-Torki – (above) is remarkable of its kind. Suspended six storeys above the street by a complex and carefully calculated sequence of cantilevers and crobels, this striking chamber was where the whole family gathered together to enjoy the cooling onshore breezes.
Left From beneath, a merchant's house presents the familiar combination of grandeur and intimacy.

Many of the balconies and bay windows – indeed any of the wooden supports and facades – of Jeddah's historic houses, are constructed of teak or similar hardwoods, imported from further east but worked by local carpenters, carvers and turners.

In past times – as today – it was the prosperous mercantile community that provided the patronage for the craftsmen which in our times makes Jeddah so notable a city. The Royal Family also encourages traditional crafts.

Ornately carved bay windows are usually not glazed, to allow the circulation of cool air. Glass was not worth the problems of transportation.

In high summer, before the days of air conditioning, rawashin *made life tolerable for the Jeddah citizen.*

The past builders of Jeddah naturally relied on available materials. With no good quality building stone, coral limestone – though porous and comparatively soft – was the natural answer.

Mosques are immediately in reach of every citizen. Left *The Hanefi mosque, on the western side of King Faisal Street, has a particularly prominent eight-sided minaret divided into six levels. Immediately below and bottom, the coral built Mimar mosque still has its original doors. Right The Al-Falah school with its striking onion dome sheathed in timber is Jeddah's most ancient surviving boys' school.*

The villa bearing the family name of Beit Bajnaid (see pages 14 & 15), though substantially modified from its original conception, is well endowed with carving, fretwork, lattices, ironwork, verandahs and galleries. It is a significant candidate for restoration (the two top pictures, above right and opposite). Below left, its near contemporary, once a merchant's house, was also a foreign embassy.

The intention is to eliminate the motor vehicle from substantial areas of the old city, and, for the sake of the local inhabitants, to establish pedestrian precincts and piazzas wherever possible. Though the old town is no more than 1.5 square kilometres, its population is 41,000 of whom 81 per cent, according to a recent poll, preferred to continue living in the old city, because of "its links with the past." A total of 550 old buildings are scheduled for preservation and rehabilitation in the city's historic core.

Right: *Gabil Street, heart of a Suq, in a quiet moment. Suqs today are paved and elegantly covered. The Municipality's priority was to extend throughout the old town the basic facilities.*

In the labyrinth of shops and businesses are to be found enterprises of extraordinary wealth and diversity. Shopkeepers with modest premises may be dealing in millions of rials and travelling all over the world.

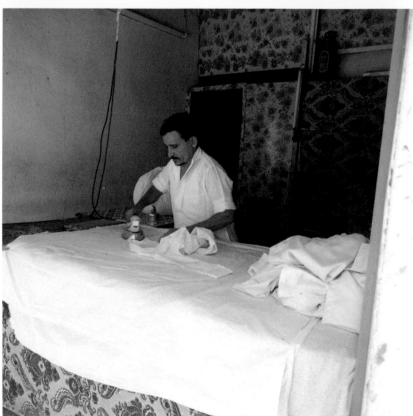

JEDDAH TODAY AND TOMORROW

As the country's dominant international commercial centre, Jeddah has been host to the world's banks longer than anywhere else in the Kingdom. Above left The Samman Centre, in the Hamra district, houses a branch of the Cairo Bank. Above and opposite The Riyad Bank, the Saudi-French Bank, the Saudi-British Bank and the National Commercial Bank are among the many international financial institutions with major premises in the Old Town's commercial area, which may be regarded as the seedbed of the country's business enterprise.

By night the lights of the heart of the city give evidence of its vigour and variety. *Opposite* Offices and hotels light up the front of the Old Town along part of the lagoon shoreline. *Right* One of the training centres of Saudia, the national airline, headquartered in Jeddah, presents an expanding silhouette. *Below* The famous contours of the Khozam water tower, like a luminous bi-valve, contrast with the imperiousness of the Khozam Palace's equally celebrated gateway.

Above *Jeddah's citizens sometimes express their loyalty in lights – as with this archway across the road from Mecca congratulating King Khalid on his restoration to health.*

82

The city's intellectual life is focused upon King Abdul Aziz University (right, right centre and below centre), *situated on the eastern side of the city, and site of study nuclei such as the Hajj Research Centre.*

Medical care is provided by Government hospitals and private hospitals, as above and right – *with enough hospital beds for every citizen that needs one.*

Opposite, top *The old city centre's skyline from the sea presents a wholly modern image.*

One of downtown Jeddah's first essays in modern architecture was the Commercial and Residential Centre, popularly known as the Queen's Building (left and above), in King Abdul Aziz Street.

One of the largest apartment block complexes (this page), popularly known as Jeddah Towers, has a capacity for 10,000 people – some two thousand families. Also completed in 1980 was the Bin Laden office block (opposite), in Al Sharafiya, whose architects chose simple lines and plain surfaces to achieve their effect.

Jeddah's major business offices are centred along the waterfront of the old city. Many rise out of land reclaimed from the sea – among them the Bugshan Centre (below) and the National Commercial Bank complex (left and opposite). Overleaf: *The hills that ring the city are visible as dawn spreads across the south-eastern part of the city, dominated by the water tower. The photograph is taken from the roof of the Wasahlan Meridien hotel, whose tented* al fresco *restaurant is seen* inset.

The city's religious life is catered for by an abundance of mosques, some modest in scale, some full of grandeur like the Khozam Palace mosque, some expressing an individual grace and serenity.

The Corniche mosque, one of the three set as pavilions along the coast, received the Aga Khan Award for Architecture in 1989. The prayer hall with the Mihrab (left) is based on a plan where the prayer hall occupies most of the space. The simple yet visually effective outline of the minaret and dome is silhouetted against the sky (right). Prince Salman's mosque (below) makes brilliant use of Jeddah's woodworkers.

The Hajj Terminal's total area of 430,000 square metres makes it 25 per cent larger than the world's largest office building, the Pentagon in Washington. It includes prayer and rest areas, restaurants, shops, banks and post offices. The terminal was completed in 1982 and can comfortably cope with the one million Hajj pilgrims expected annually this decade. After the pilgrims arrive at the twin building complexes of the Hajj Terminal (top) they walk through an enclosed air-conditioned processing area (above centre) manned by Saudia staff. The Hajj Terminal can hold up to 80,000 Hajjis (above and right) during the peak pilgrimage period and they can now choose whether to visit Jeddah or travel directly to Makkah from the airport.

*During the annual Hajj pilgrimage Jeddah becomes vividly cosmopolitan.
Above right Pilgrims from Morocco, part of a royal retinue, are given an
official escort. Above, top and right Pilgrims from South Asia and
West Africa express their thankfulness, in prayer and joy, upon setting
foot in the "heartland" of Islam. Opposite Special accommodation for
pilgrims is provided at various points in the city region.*

Since the early 1970s, the national airline, Saudia, has been the fastest growing airline in the world, and Jeddah itself the busiest communications centre in the Middle East. It is now the site of the Middle East's largest and most modern airport.

Overleaf *While the merchant ships of the world converge on Jeddah, a local fisherman – whose ancestors were similarly occupied two and a half thousand years ago in the same place – provides the city with fresh fish.*

Top *Jeddah port provides a forty-eight-hour turnaround for unloading vehicles. The city is the principal point of distribution for goods – e.g. cars (above) or meat (right).*

The Municipality provides a modern fish market and uniformed fish cleaners (above and below).

Jeddah's heavy industries, occupying some five per cent of its total area, range from water desalination (above), *coupled with electricity generation, and concrete* (left), *to steel works, and oil refining* (right).

Light industry includes mattress-making (left) and highly skilled woodwork. Above and right New homes on Palestine Street (Shara Filistin) set the vogue in use of exquisite Jeddah-crafted woodwork, also used to restore the former British Legation (right) where T. E. Lawrence lodged in 1916 – now to become a restaurant.

Imaginative planning makes the most of Jeddah's seafront, with the fine Corniche road (right) giving onto the sea for many miles, northwards and southwards. At the heart of the city the lagoon (below and left) plays its benign role, with roads and waterways and pedestrian precincts to bring its influence to bear on citizens. Civic pride is encouraged (right) but prevails of its own accord.

*A watersports complex along the Baghdadiya
shore* (left and top) *provides for Jeddah's many* *aquatic enthusiasts, as do three modern stadia
for footballers.*

The impressive Mahmal Centre in the heart of Jeddah includes a seven-storey shopping mall linked by a high-level bridge to a twenty-storey office block (top). Sophistication also characterises the shopping precincts of downtown King Abdul Aziz Street (above).

A car manufacturer's showroom (above) makes modern use of oriental ideas.

Oriental splendour is today put to good use by appealing to the vanities of the shopper in a Hamra shop appealing to "the top of the market".

On Baghdadiya Street a customer can select from examples of the world's finest jewellery (above and top).

While various large shopping centres exist in the city, shops of every size, speciality and income level cater for a cosmopolitan spending public.

Left One of the major shopping complexes in the city is the Jeddah Shopping Centre, on the Medina Road. Others include Caravan and Redec Plaza.

Jeddah's population in 1980 was already near one million, and was expected to reach 1.6 million ten years later and 2.25 million by the end of the century. While villas of individual character, like that of Anaykish (right), remain a popular form of residence many citizens make their home in one of the modern blocks of flats or housing complexes (below), often clad in marble and including interesting use of wood.

Opposite, the self-contained suburb of Khaldiya – popularly known as Saudia City – in the north of the city area, has a population of 14,000, of whom many heads of family work for the national airline.

Jeddah's homes of aristocratic and mercantile
families demonstrate some of the most
imaginatively successful private building in the
modern world. Many of them are close to the
sea, in the Hamra and Mosadiya districts.

The vigorous ideas developed by private householders have helped to stimulate the originality of design of housing estates and apartment blocks alike. Housing will represent some twenty-nine per cent of metropolitan Jeddah's anticipated 1,215 square kilometres.

Arab and Islamic styles are successfully blended with the modern lines of recent buildings. Saudi Arabian Marketing and Refining Company – SAMAREC – is headquartered on a landscaped area in the Mosadia district just west of the Madinah Road (opposite top). *Government buildings exampled here are all in the Al Hamra district; the Ministry of Planning* (opposite bottom), *the Ministry of the Interior* (left) *and the Youth Affairs Jeddah headquarters* (above). *Government and community buildings will represent some 3.7 per cent of metropolitan Jeddah, under the evolving master plan.*

Jeddah's princely palaces demonstrate the successful evolution of a distinctly Arab modern architectural character, from the Guest Palace, top, *to the recent senior Prince's palace* (above) *and new Royal palace* (opposite).

Once the colour of the dun landscape in which it is set, Jeddah today is increasingly green. A botanical garden was under construction in the early 1980s, as well as a "Desert Park" south-east of the city.

The Jeddah public is efficiently served by the national bus line, SAPTCO – the Saudi Arabian Public Transport Company (left). Separate sections of each coach are allocated to male and female passengers.

Jeddah's plant consciousness is reflected in the metal sculpture (right) by Giovanni, on Shara Al Emir Fahd bin Abdul Aziz (Shara Sitteen).

Overleaf The sculptural creation of Julio Lafuente, with its ship motif (backed up by a stanza of poetry), is assembled on the Corniche (see also page 1).

Jeddah has grown celebrated for its cheerfully imaginative public monuments and sculpture. Above, a little square off Shara Khalid bin Al Walid is brought alive at night by a sculptured fountain by Saudi sculptor Shafiq Mazloom.

The Lafuente sculpture (top) dominates a roundabout near the industrial area, in the city's southern district. Above, the city's initial letter is represented in cast iron on the Corniche. Left Sacks of flour announce the function of a supermarket.

Left *The silhouetted globe, in Hamra, was one of Jeddah's first sculptures.*

Centre left, above: *An appropriate motif of fish by Giovanni, and* far left, *a boat by Cashella;* middle left, *Arnoldo Pomadero's globe. The column,* left, *shows the waning of the moon.* Above and top right *are works by Lafuente.*

129

The wide sweep of the Corniche area north of the city, set aside for recreation of the citizenry, provides the opportunities for arresting the eye with unusual and sometimes witty public sculpture. Right: *the remains of Jeddah's thundering* kindasah *(condenser) from which the townsmen of a couple of generations ago first extracted fresh water from the sea, and* opposite, *the "monument to the unknown cyclist" of the same period.*

Fishermen's nets and the date palms provide the theme for two fine public sculptures **above.** *Right, "Poets' Garden" is adorned with the work of Saudi sculptor Abdul Hatim Radwi.*

Centre left, *a Henry Moore stands beside the Corniche road across the Lagoon. Left Jeddah's earliest coast guard motor boats are preserved as monuments for posterity.*

A scatter of birds make a fine monument, as do Lafuente's ewers, on a Hamra roadside (above), recalling the familiar vessels in which fresh water was carefully preserved in past times.

A shell-like form (with which the shore abounds) inspired the sculptor far left, *and an entwined motif* centre. *The aircraft, preserved in the design by Lafuente, near the old airport buildings, is believed to be the first to have operated regularly from Jeddah's original airfield in the mid-1940s.*

135

The drawings on the following pages demonstrate the direction of the city's future development, particularly in the fusion of modern developmental ideas into the traditional areas of the city. All drawings of things to come represent schemes approved by the Municipality.

Right *A piazza in the northern part of the Old Town today, off King Faisal Street, is contrasted with the same area after renewal.*

Below *Here the drawings,* left and right, *contrast a piazza, now and in the future, in the Bab Mecca area on the eastern perimeter of the Old Town.*

The purpose of rebuilding Bab Makkah – the former gateway in the old city wall, opening onto the Makkah Road – as it was before it was demolished during the early phase of the city's expansion, is to create the pedestrianised area right. Below is seen the result of plans for the south side of the Reza Centre, downtown.

With water provided from the desalination of sea water, gardens have multiplied throughout the city, both public – as, for instance, that of the old Foreign Ministry (left) *and neighbouring Poet's Garden* (top) *and private Garden* (immediately above).

*An element of Islamic fantasy is superbly exemplified in Al-Hamra by the
museum built to preserve the material culture of Arabia and the Middle East.*

Work on Jeddah's King Abduli Aziz's Airport started in 1974 and it took eight years to complete this project, considered to be an international milestone in the history of both aviation and architecture. Saudi was already handling nearly eight million passengers in the late 1970s: the airport is now ten times larger than was originally envisaged at the planning stage in 1973 and covers over forty square miles. The Italian marble of the magnificent Hajj Terminal buildings (far left and left) reflects the dazzling white ceilng and complements a large ornamental pool and fountains. Its two aprons together can hold 20 Boeing 747s and some 24 other aircraft in more remote parking positions.